BUT GOD
A JOURNEY OF PAIN,,
PURPOSE AND RESILIENCE

APOSTLE DR. KEN FULLER

Jeremiah 29:11

[11] *For I know the thoughts that I think toward you, saith the Lord, thoughts of peace, and not of evil, to give you an expected end.*

Table of Contents

Book dedication

This book, But God: A Journey of Pain, Purpose, and Resilience, is dedicated to two extraordinary people who have profoundly shaped my life.

To my mother, Shirley Fuller, whose unwavering strength and boundless love have been a guiding light in my darkest moments. And to my best friend since the 4th grade, Deacon Markeith Reynolds, whose steadfast faith and perseverance continue to inspire me daily.

You both embody resilience, determination, and grace. I have witnessed your trials, admired your resolve, and marveled at the power of But God in your lives.

This is for you.

Introduction

Life is a tapestry woven with threads of chaos, perseverance, faith, and redemption. Each chapter of our journey tells a story—a story of love that refuses to give up, of storms that threaten to consume us, and of a God who transforms pain into purpose.

This book reflects my life, lived through trials and triumphs, revealing the unwavering faith that became a lifeline in the darkest moments. It begins with the unbreakable bond of my mother's love, planting seeds of resilience even in the midst of chaos. From the projects of Englewood to forging a path of perseverance, each step is marked by growth and transformation.

Together, we walk through fires of adversity, turbulent adolescent challenges, and the weight of rebellion that yields redemption. Seasons of love, loss, and profound lessons remind us that even in pain, there is purpose. As a single pastor navigating ministry, I've wrestled with storms and crises that tested every fiber of my faith. Yet, through it all, I found a God who never abandoned me.

This is more than my story—it is a testament to the human spirit and the divine grace that sustains us. Each chapter is a beacon of hope, a reminder that no matter how fierce the storm, we are never without an anchor.

By the final chapter, you'll see that it is not the absence of trials that defines us, but how we rise from the ashes. With every setback, there is a comeback. With every pain, a divine purpose. And with every storm, a lesson that strengthens us for the journey ahead.

This book is an invitation to find faith in the fire, resilience in the rubble, and hope in heartbreak. Together, let us embark on this journey of perseverance and redemption, discovering that with God, the story is never over.

About the Author

Apostle Dr. Ken Fuller, a father of five, believes ministry begins at home, grounding his faith and leadership in family.

After high school, he joined the Marine Corps, learning that "pain is weakness leaving the body." This principle fueled his success in corporate America, where he excelled in management, engineering, and project management, earning certifications like Lean Six Sigma.

At 12, Dr. Ken was called to preach the Gospel. Ordained under the late Rev. Dr. Annie R. Sconier, he completed ministerial studies at New Thought Development Center of Chicago. In 2012, he launched 1 WALK Ministries, which grew into Social Center International Ministries in 2013, a 501(c)(3) serving communities through drives, job fairs, leadership training, and partnerships addressing critical needs like health care and domestic violence. Ministries such as M.A.N. and W3 foster spiritual growth.

Dr. Ken, a pastor to pastors and community activist, travels nationwide spreading the Gospel, mentoring leaders, and teaching through platforms like *Chopping It Up with Apostle Ken* and *The Word Tavern*, which evolved into the School of the Word Institute.

In 2023, he earned an Honorary Doctor of Divinity and Christian Leadership from the School of the Great Commission Bible College.

Today, Dr. Ken pastors, teaches, and leads with grace, rebuilding communities and inspiring growth. Social Center International Ministries remains a place for family, community, and transformation.

Chapter1: From Chaos to Faith: A Mother's Love and the Seeds of Resilience

For years, the words of Isaiah 40:30 rang in my ears: "Even the youths shall faint and be weary, and the young men shall utterly fall." While the verse continues, this portion always resonated deeply with me. It described a truth that I would come to know intimately in my own life—a truth about strength, weariness, and the enduring power of faith.

I grew up at 4950 S. State Street in Chicago, a place bustling with life, energy, and the sounds of community. My home was filled with the presence of my mother, my seven siblings, and my stepfather. For a child, life seemed simple, even joyful. The world outside our doors may have had its share of struggles, but within the walls of our home, there was love, warmth, and a sense of stability that I cherished deeply.

We didn't know what hunger or financial hardship truly felt like during those early years. Holidays like Thanksgiving and Christmas were magical times. Our table overflowed with food, laughter echoed through the house, and the air was rich with the aroma of traditional dishes. My siblings and I would play games, share stories, and revel in the happiness that seemed boundless.

My parents, like any couple, had their ups and downs, but to us, their love provided a foundation. Their relationship wasn't perfect, but it was real and enduring—or so it seemed. I saw my stepfather as a cornerstone of our family, a figure who, though not my biological father, treated us as his own. Our home was alive with love, and for a time, it felt unshakable.

 But life, as I would come to learn, is seldom without its trials. Every good thing faces challenges, and sometimes those challenges redefine the very fabric of our existence. My greatest heartbreak as a child came the day my stepfather moved out.

I was too young to understand the complexities of adult relationships, but I knew one thing for sure: his absence left a void. He was still the father of my youngest brother, and he tried to remain involved in some capacity, but the dynamic of our household changed forever.

Even with four brothers—three older and one younger—there was something about a father's presence that felt irreplaceable. His departure shifted the balance in our home. My mother did her best to hold things together, but I could sense the strain in her eyes and her voice. The weight of being both mother and father to eight children fell heavily on her shoulders.

As if to mirror the changes within our family, the world outside began to shift as well. The projects we called home became increasingly dangerous. Violence, once an abstract concept, became a tangible reality. The first time I heard a gunshot, I was just a child, no older than five or six.

The sound was loud, sharp, and jarring. I didn't understand how something so small—a single bullet—could carry such devastating power, taking lives and shattering families. That moment planted a seed of fear within me, a fear that grew with each passing day.

I began to worry incessantly. What if one of my family members was caught in the cross-fire? What if a stray bullet took them away from me? These questions haunted my young mind, turning innocence into anxiety.

Despite being a child, free from the burdens of bills and adult responsibilities, I carried this invisible weight. The chaos outside—shouting, sirens, running footsteps—etched itself into my memory. The world no longer felt safe.

At home, I began to notice changes in my mother. The laughter that once filled our house was replaced by quiet moments of reflection. I would find her sitting in silence, her face etched with worry. One night, I overheard her talking to someone.

The walls in the projects were thin, but her voice was muffled. I couldn't make out the words, but it was clear she was confiding in someone. I wondered who it could be. A friend? A neighbor? A family member? Not long after, she introduced us to someone who would change our lives forever: God.

At nearly six years old, I was introduced to Jesus Christ. My mother, in the midst of her struggles, had found solace in faith. She decided we were going to church—a concept I didn't understand at the time. My aunt and cousin, through marriage, had connected her to a church called Victory in Christ Spiritual Church.

One Sunday, she gathered all of us, dressed us in our best clothes, and prepared us for what would be our first church experience.

I still remember the process vividly. She heated the iron on the stove to straighten my sisters' hair, shined our faces with Vaseline until they gleamed, and combed down the boys' hair neatly. We looked polished, ready for something important—something special.

We boarded the State Street bus, then transferred to the 59th Street bus, which took us to the church on 59th and Morgan. The pastor, Bishop Nephus White, greeted us warmly.

 The service began with Sunday school, where children and adults learned about God and the story of Jesus Christ. At first, it was quiet and structured, almost like a classroom. But when the main service began, everything changed.

People sang with fervor, their voices rising to the heavens. Some cried, others testified, and Bishop White preached with passion and conviction. The energy in the room was overwhelming but uplifting. For the first time, I began to feel the weight of my fear and anxiety lift, replaced by a sense of hope.

This gathering of believers felt like a refuge, a safe haven amidst the chaos of the world outside. I realized that this was who my mother had been talking to during her quiet moments at night. It was strange, yet comforting. By the end of the service, I felt a spark of hope—a sense that maybe, just maybe, everything could be okay.

After church, we stayed for the fellowship meal. For a child, this was perhaps the highlight of the day. The food was delicious, and the people were kind. From that day forward, church became a regular part of our lives.

 Back at home, Mom's faith continued to grow. She talked to God daily, prayed over us, and led by example. But as the crime in our neighborhood worsened, she made a bold decision.

With unwavering trust in God, she moved us to a new neighborhood in Englewood, on the South Side of Chicago. We left behind the familiarity of the projects and ventured into the unknown. Our new home on 57th and Aberdeen marked the beginning of a new chapter.

This move wasn't easy. We had to adjust to a new environment, new neighbors, and new routines. But through it all, one thing remained constant: Mom's faith. Her trust in God reassured us that everything would be all right, even when the future felt uncertain.

Looking back, I realize how pivotal those early years were in shaping who I would become. Life in the projects, the sound of gunshots, and the introduction to faith all worked together to lay the foundation for my journey.

The projects taught me about the realities of life—the challenges, the fears, and the importance of community. The church introduced me to hope, faith, and the transformative power of God's love. And my mother's resilience showed me what it means to persevere, even in the face of adversity.

As Isaiah 40:30 reminds us, even the strongest among us can grow weary. But through faith and perseverance, we find the resilience to keep going. My mother's faith taught me that, and it's a lesson I carry with me to this day.

Over the years, I've come to understand that life is a series of challenges and triumphs. There will be moments of joy and moments of sorrow, but it is often in our darkest times that we find the greatest strength.

My mother's decision to turn to God wasn't just an act of faith—it was an act of love. She knew that she couldn't shield us from every hardship, but she could introduce us to a source of strength greater than ourselves.

That introduction changed my life. It taught me that faith isn't about having all the answers; it's about trusting in God's plan, even when we don't understand it.

Today, as I reflect on those formative years, I am filled with gratitude. Gratitude for my mother, who showed me what it means to trust in God. Gratitude for the church, which became a sanctuary for our family. And gratitude for the lessons learned through both joy and hardship.

The words of Isaiah 40:30 continue to resonate with me. They serve as a reminder that we all have moments of weariness, moments when we feel like giving up. But it is in those moments that we must turn to our faith, drawing strength from the God who never grows weary.

As I navigate the challenges of adulthood, I carry these lessons with me. They remind me that no matter how difficult life may seem, there is always hope. And that hope, rooted in faith, is the greatest gift of all.

Chapter 2 From Projects to Perseverance: Our Journey to Englewood

It's official: the family has moved to the South Side of Chicago from 4950 S. State, and now we are living in Englewood. This new beginning brought with it both excitement and uncertainty. We live next door to my auntie, who was a big reason for Mom bringing us to this area. Auntie was also the one who introduced Mom to the local church, which would soon become a central part of our lives.

We went from living in a cramped two-bedroom apartment in the projects to a spacious two-flat brownstone. We lived on the first floor and the landlord lived on the second floor.

Our new home had three bedrooms, a large living area, a kitchen, and even a backyard. The porch out front became a gathering spot, and the neighborhood was filled with families. Kids ran up and down the streets in a way that felt so different from the echoing halls of the projects.

In the projects, we played in narrow corridors and relied on elevators to get to the ground floor. Now, we had open streets and yards to explore—a new freedom that was as thrilling as it was unfamiliar. The space felt like a fresh canvas, a place where life could be rewritten.

This move also meant new challenges. It was time for me to start school, and the separation anxiety hit hard. I was so used to being surrounded by my family that the thought of spending six hours a day away from them felt unbearable.

I cried and struggled to adjust, but slowly, I began to find my footing. My teachers noticed my hesitancy and did their best to make me feel at home, but it wasn't until I made friends that I started to see school as more than just a place I had to go.

 Englewood was a community where everyone seemed to know everyone. We had a store nearby called the Davis Store, where the owner trusted the neighborhood so much that he allowed families to get groceries on credit.

Mom would sometimes send us with a note—a makeshift invoice—for items we needed, when she was in between pay periods or money was funny;, promising to pay on her next payday. That kind of trust and closeness was the fabric of our new life.

 Mom always emphasized the importance of respecting adults and heeding their guidance, especially when they were steering us in the right direction. Her firm discipline, coupled with the vigilant presence of our uncles, aunties, grandmother, and her close friends, ensured we were raised with strong values.

Our sense of community transcended the walls of our home, weaving through the streets we walked, the neighbors we greeted, and the local stores and parks we frequented. Everyone played a part in shaping us, and it often felt as though the entire neighborhood was united in their hope for our success.

The church was another anchor. Victory in Christ Spiritual Church was about a five- to eight-minute walk from our home. Each Sunday, Mom made sure we were dressed to perfection. Our faces shined with vaseline, and the girls had their hair straightened. Occasionally, the pastor would pick us up in the church van, but most Sundays, we walked together—Mom, my seven siblings, and me.

Mom joined the choir, and it wasn't long before she became the choir director. My auntie Mary was one of the lead singers, and the songs we sang—"Victory Shall Be Mine," "Trouble in My Way," and "Precious Lord, Take My Hand"—filled the sanctuary with hope. My grandmother, Alice Cooper, joined us when she could, singing hymns that resonated with her faith and life experiences.

The church became more than just a place of worship; it was a refuge, a place where our spirits were lifted despite the hardships we faced. Mom poured herself into her role at the church, and in doing so, she found strength that carried over into our home life. Her faith was contagious, and even as kids, we began to understand that God was central to our survival and our joy.

We were settling into this new life, but challenges soon emerged. Mom was our sole provider, doing everything she could to make ends meet. My stepdad helped sporadically, but the burden mostly fell on her shoulders. Then came a surprise: my biological father, whom I had never met, decided to start coming around.

I was thrilled at the thought of having my biological dad in my life. Every boy needs a father, and I was no exception. Mom would tell me, "Your dad will be here soon," and I would sit on the porch, dressed and ready, waiting. But too often, he wouldn't show up.

When he did show up, he didn't use the time to teach me about life, money, or what it meant to be a man. Instead, he had me do physical labor, which felt more like a task than an opportunity to bond. His inconsistency cut deep, leaving me questioning my own worth.

I couldn't help but think about when my step-father moved out, and the question lingered in my mind: *What was it about me that made the men in my life walk away?*

 By this time, I was eight, going on 9 and the weight of these experiences began to shape my view of the world. But even amid this pain, the love of my mom and siblings, and our faith in God, helped me endure. I clung to the lessons we learned at church and the songs of hope that filled our home.

 Still, life in Englewood wasn't easy. As we grew older, the struggles became harder to ignore. Shoes developed holes before we could afford new ones, and bullies at school from time to time would tease kids with holes in their shoes. I learned to walk carefully to hide the damage, but the humiliation lingered.

Our financial difficulties deepened. There were times when the lights, gas, and water were shut off. Mom, ever resourceful, found ways to keep us afloat. She borrowed water from my aunt's house and used kerosene heaters to keep us warm during winter.

One winter evening, Mom asked me to grab a pot of cabbage from my aunt's house, that she had prepared earlier. It was a snowy day and as I began to walk with the cabbage and walk up the stairs, I slipped on the icy steps, spilling the food everywhere.

Mom came out, and seeing our dinner scattered across the ground, she broke down in tears. That moment was seared into my memory. I prayed to God, asking for strength to help my mom one day.

Despite everything, Mom never lost her faith. She would sing hymns late into the night, her voice filled with conviction. Our pastor often reminded us that the closer we got to God, the harder the enemy would work to break us. But Mom held on, and so did we.

During one of our darkest winters, with no utilities and only kerosene heaters to warm us, Mom sang at church: "I'll let nothing separate me from the love of God." Her faith inspired us to believe that breakthrough was just around the corner.

Though it felt like we were at rock bottom, Mom taught us resilience. She reminded us that God had kept us safe in the projects, and He would see us through this, too. Those words became a mantra, a source of comfort when everything else seemed to fail.

As time went on, glimmers of hope began to emerge. Mom had a special way with people—she never met a stranger and was always willing to lend a hand to anyone in need. Her kindness left an impression on those around her, and people remembered it. Small blessings started to find their way to us: a family member lending support, or a friend stepping in just when we needed it most. These gestures, though they may have seemed minor at the time, became lifelines that reminded us we were never truly alone.

 Englewood was a complicated place. It was a mix of love and struggle, community and hardship. But it was also where we grew stronger, where we learned that faith and perseverance could carry us through anything. It was where I began to understand the power of resilience—not just as a concept, but as a way of life.

Every setback, every heartbreak, and every challenge became a stepping stone toward something greater. Looking back, I realize that those years in Englewood were some of the most formative of my life. They taught me that even when the world feels heavy, there is always light to be found. Sometimes, it's in a hymn sung in the dark. Sometimes, it's in the laughter of a sibling And sometimes, it's in the quiet strength of a mother who refuses to give up.

 That strength, that resilience, and that unshakable faith are lessons I carry with me to this day. They are reminders that no matter how hard life gets, there is always a way through. And for that, I will always be grateful.

Chapter 3 Faith Through the Fire

Mom's prayers, her unwavering faith in God, and her resilience had finally paid off. A long-time friend from her childhood, who lived just down the block, offered us an upstairs apartment at the end of the street. For Mom, this was a victory—a chance to rebuild her confidence after the challenges we had faced. I silently prayed that she didn't see herself as a failure because of the trials we had endured.

Over time, I came to understand a valuable truth: sometimes bad things happen to good people, and it's no reflection of their worth.

We found ourselves in a new neighborhood, though still within the same community—this was now our second move on the same block. As I mentioned before, we had recently come through a tough season of financial hardship. It felt like we had finally overcome, but life has a way of throwing new challenges at you. That's why staying prayed up is essential.

This time, the challenge wasn't just personal—it was systemic. The crack cocaine epidemic swept through black communities like a hurricane, leaving devastation in its wake. It tore apart families, communities, and lives. Some of the people in our community—who were once working-class husbands, wives, friends, and neighbors—fell victim to addiction or became entangled in drug sales. For those of us who steered clear of either, the focus became prayer and vigilance.

The drug trade brought gang violence with it, and drive-by shootings became terrifyingly frequent. Tragically, the bullets often missed their intended targets, claiming the lives of innocent bystanders. There's no sound like the wail of a mother who has lost her child to senseless violence—it is a cry that cuts straight to the soul.

As a young black teenager-a male, this environment shaped me in ways I didn't fully understand at the time. The anxiety of walking down the street, unsure whether the next passing car with tinted windows would bring trouble, was a constant weight. Yet even amidst the chaos, Mom remained steadfast in her faith, urging us to trust God and push forward.

One incident stands out vividly in my memory. My sister had gone to the park with some friends, and while she was there, a member of a gang called the Bogus Boys threw something at her, hitting her. She came home in tears, distraught and scared. Mom, ever the protector, grabbed a baseball bat and headed straight to the park, barefoot and ready to defend her child.

 My siblings and I followed her, watching as she fearlessly confronted the group of young men. She demanded to know who had hurt her daughter. When one of the gang members identified the culprit, I immediately confronted him, and a fight broke out.

It was chaotic—there were so many of them—but the beautiful part was how the community rallied around us. Neighbors we knew stepped in to break up the fight, pulling people away and standing with us. That day, our community came together in solidarity, declaring that enough was enough.

I'd be lying if I said I wasn't scared. These were people known for their involvement in drugs and violence, and I didn't know how things would end. But God's grace and protection surrounded us. His love kept us through that storm, reminding me that survival wasn't just about physical safety—it was about keeping our integrity intact.

Temptation loomed large during those years. With money tight and opportunities scarce, the allure of quick cash from illegal activities was strong. Friends of mine were already caught up in that world, and I often found myself wrestling with the idea of following them.

I wanted to ease my family's struggles, to give my mom the life she deserved. Yet, whenever

I was on the verge of stepping into something wrong, one particular friend-which is the deacon of the ministry today, would intervene. He'd tell me, "This isn't for you. Go home." He'd remind me that I had a calling on my life, that God had something greater for me.

But I couldn't help wondering: If God had something greater for me, why did it feel like my family, and I were always struggling? Why did it seem like we were the ones left wanting, while others thrived—even if their success came through dubious means?

One thing I've learned over time is that not every good-looking opportunity is a God-ordained one. The enemy has a way of dressing up traps to look like blessings. Those moments of temptation taught me the importance of discernment and the strength of community.

Despite the chaos, there were bright moments in our neighborhood. We cherished block parties, played softball in the alley, and cooled off under the spray of fire hydrants. But as we grew older, life became more complicated.

We moved again, this time to a home on Garfield Boulevard, but still in Englewood. By then, many of us were entering adulthood. My siblings graduated from high school, went to prom, and began carving out their own paths. My older sister married and moved to Texas, though she eventually returned.

We also faced profound loss during this time. Our family matriarch, my grandmother Alice B. Cooper, passed away. Her death shook us, forcing us to adjust and find strength in one another. It was a season of highs and lows, yet our faith remained our anchor.

Looking back, I see that God's hand was with us through it all. His faithfulness didn't mean we were spared from hardship, but it gave us the strength to endure. Through the tears, the trials, and even the triumphs, we held on to the belief that better days were ahead. And as Mom always reminded us, faith wasn't just about surviving—it was about trusting in a God who sees, knows, and ultimately provides.

One of the greatest blessings during those years was the community that surrounded us. Englewood may have been fraught with challenges, but it was also filled with people who looked out for one another.

The local church became our second home. Victory in Christ Spiritual Church wasn't just a place of worship; it was a sanctuary. Mom became deeply involved, joining the choir and later leading it as the director. She poured her heart into songs like "Victory Shall Be Mine" and "Trouble in My Way," which resonated deeply with our lived experiences.

The church wasn't just about faith; it was about action. When families in the neighborhood were in need, the congregation would rally together to provide food, clothing, or simply a listening ear. I can't tell you how many times the pastor, Bishop Nephus White blessed people and never said anything about it.

As I reflect on those years, I realize how much they shaped who I am today. They taught me the value of resilience, the power of faith, and the importance of community. I learned that life's hardships don't define you; how you respond to them does.

Mom's unwavering faith became my foundation. Even in the darkest moments, her belief in God's provision never wavered. Her prayers sustained us, her resilience inspired us, and her love held us together.

Today, I carry those lessons with me, knowing that the fire we walked through wasn't just about survival—it was about preparation. It refined us, strengthened us, and ultimately brought us closer to God.

In the end, faith through the fire became not just a lesson but a lifestyle. It's a reminder that no matter how intense the flames, God's presence is always with us. He doesn't promise a life free of trials, but He does promise to walk with us through them.

Mom's life, and our family's journey, is a testament to that promise. This will continue to speak volumes for many years and generations to come.

Chapter 4 Adolescent Challenges and Growth

Navigating the hallways of high school, I found myself on the cusp of adulthood, wrestling with the complexities of identity and the chaotic waves of puberty. At just twelve years old, I stumbled into my first attempted sexual encounter, utterly unprepared for what lay ahead. The aftermath left me bewildered, questioning my understanding of intimacy and what it meant to connect with another person on such a profound level.

Soon, I discovered that I was engaged in a tug-of-war with my own desires, battling the allure of pornography while grappling with the confusing sensations my body was experiencing.

In moments of introspection, I began to recognize the importance of prayer—not merely for physical needs like food on the table or financial stability, but for the hidden internal struggles that often remained unspoken. I learned that we must also pray for our private battles, the things that evoke shame despite their enticing nature.

This tumultuous period of my life revealed a significant void; I yearned for a father figure to guide me through these uncharted waters. My stepfather was present, yet the comfort to share my deepest struggles with him eluded me. The storm of adolescence felt like a journey I had to weather on my own, without the support I so desperately craved.

Fast forward to my senior year; excitement filled the air as I prepared for prom with my first official girlfriend. I was fortunate enough to be somewhat popular, actively participating in various activities like homecoming court, the drama club, and the Afro club. I had a sense of belonging that made my high school experience memorable, but the underlying insecurities still loomed large.

On prom day, although I had just received my driver's license, I couldn't drive myself. My older brother and his girlfriend, a nurse, graciously took us to the event, which only added to the excitement.

Prom night carried an unspoken expectation among young boys—that intimacy would naturally follow the dance. After the prom, my date and I went to a family member's house where we spent the night together. In a moment that was both exhilarating and overwhelming, we crossed a line I had never anticipated.

To my shock, blood stained the sheets, leaving both of us embarrassed and confused. I assumed it was something I had done wrong, a mistake on my part that I couldn't comprehend.

The next morning, my family member reassured me, explaining that my girlfriend had simply started her menstrual cycle. I had never even heard the term "cycle" before, and my innocent inquiry about whether boys had cycles too elicited laughter from the adults in the room.

Though my girlfriend struggled with the embarrassment of the situation, we navigated through it together, forging a bond that, despite the awkwardness, felt significant. These moments were formative; I was beginning to grasp the complexities of life and the learning curve that accompanied growing up.

With prom behind me, graduation arrived, yet clarity about my future still eluded me. The transition from high school to adulthood is often filled with uncertainty, and I was no exception. Shortly after graduating, my girlfriend and I decided to part ways, recognizing the youthful nature of our relationship. We remained friends, but it was clear that our paths were diverging. Meanwhile, I began working a regular job, attempting to figure out my path in life. I enrolled in an accelerated training course for computer operations, merely keeping busy while searching for direction.

During this period, I met the mother of my first daughter. Our connection was instantaneous; we clicked as if we had known each other for years. We spent every waking moment together, resembling a young couple in deep commitment. Despite her mother's disapproval, we were determined to stay together, even saving up a mere $325 to buy a car.

Ignoring my stepdad's advice against the purchase, I went ahead, drawn by the car's outward appearance, oblivious to the internal issues it harbored. This decision became a metaphor for life: appearances can be deceiving, and neglecting internal growth can lead to unforeseen consequences.

At 19, we made an impulsive decision to try for a baby. We didn't seek guidance or prayer; it was a choice made hastily and without foresight. The emotional rollercoaster began when attempts to conceive resulted in negative pregnancy tests, leaving me devastated each time. Each failed attempt was a painful reminder of my naivety, and I wished I had possessed the wisdom I now carry. I often found myself questioning if I was ready to become a father, and the weight of that realization bore down on me.

Eventually, we succeeded in becoming pregnant, but the joy was overshadowed by mixed reactions from our families. My mother, as always, responded with grace and prayer, while my girlfriend's mother expressed disappointment. At 19, I became a father, envisioning our future together in a perfect home filled with love and laughter. However, reality soon taught me that life seldom adheres to our dreams.

In October 1992, we welcomed our beautiful daughter into the world, and with her arrival came an avalanche of responsibilities. The moment I held her in my arms, I felt an overwhelming sense of love mixed with fear. Shortly after, my girlfriend moved to the north side of Chicago, while my mother relocated us further south of Chicago. I struggled to balance my job while embodying the role of a young father, and I faced the challenge of remaining faithful in a relationship I hadn't fully explored. The whirlwind of becoming a parent at such a young age left me feeling overwhelmed and unprepared.

As we grew apart, we clung to the hope of raising our daughter together. My girlfriend eventually moved into my mother's house, seeking support as a new mother. At 20, I felt the weight of my choices pressing down on me. Each day seemed to bring new responsibilities, and I began to question whether I was ready for this role. I realized I needed to make a change and sought direction by enlisting in the United States Marine Corps, looking for discipline and purpose.

As I underwent training, the physical distance began to strain our relationship. I received letters indicating she may have turned to other relationships while I was away, and returning home revealed some painful truths. Our once strong connection felt fragile, and the love we had shared seemed to be slipping away like sand through my fingers. We fought constantly, and my inability to communicate effectively led to toxic cycles of hurt and anger.

The toughest battle I ever fought was within my own mind, wrestling with persistent feelings of inadequacy. I found myself trapped in a cycle of comparison, measuring my worth against the successes of others. Social media at the time, was Myspace and it only amplified these struggles—endlessly scrolling through snapshots of friends' seemingly perfect lives left me feeling even more insufficient. But over time, I came to embrace a vital truth: what is meant for you will always be yours.

Each of us walks a path uniquely our own, and this understanding became a foundational piece of my growth and self-acceptance.

As I processed these experiences, I began to understand that this journey of self-discovery and growth was just beginning. The breakup hit me hard, leaving me heartbroken and unprepared for the emotional fallout. Experiencing true heartbreak for the first time felt like being hollowed out from within; a painful reminder of how love can both uplift and devastate.

The memories of our shared dreams and aspirations lingered like ghosts, pulling me back into moments we once cherished together. I couldn't bear to hear Lenny Williams' song *"Because I Love You"*. Every time the lyrics reached that heartfelt "Oh oh oh oh oh," it struck me like a tidal wave, leaving an intense knot in my stomach—a visceral reminder of all I had lost.

In the midst of this emotional turmoil, I turned to my faith for solace. Prayer became a refuge, a way for me to express my fears and hopes while seeking guidance in a time of uncertainty. I realized that while I had sought to navigate life alone, I needed to lean on my community and the support systems around me. Friends began to step in, offering their perspectives and experiences, helping me see that I wasn't alone in my struggles.

Through this process, I also began to explore my passions and interests. I took up writing as a form of therapy, pouring my thoughts and feelings onto the pages of a notebook. It became a way to articulate my journey, to make sense of the chaos that surrounded me.

Writing allowed me to reflect on my experiences, transforming my pain into something tangible. It became a form of healing, a way to reclaim my narrative and assert my identity.

As time passed, I started to embrace my role as a father fully. I made a conscious effort to be present in my daughter's life, attending her events and celebrating milestones, even amid my personal struggles. Each moment spent with her reminded me of the beauty of unconditional love and the responsibility that came with it.

I realized that being a father was about more than just providing; it was about being an active participant in her life, nurturing her growth and development.

The journey of self-discovery continued as I sought to redefine my identity beyond that of a young father. I enrolled in community college, determined to pursue my education and create a brighter future for both myself and my daughter. Balancing school, work, and parenting was no easy feat, but I was fueled by a sense of purpose. I wanted to be a role model for my daughter, demonstrating the importance of perseverance and resilience in the face of adversity.

As I delved deeper into my studies, I found subjects that ignited my passion and curiosity. I discovered a love for psychology, intrigued by the complexities of the human mind and behavior. This newfound interest prompted me to reflect on my own experiences, understanding that our struggles shape us into who we are meant to become. I began to view my past not as a series of missteps but as valuable lessons that had equipped me with the tools to navigate life's challenges.

The process of healing was gradual, marked by both setbacks and breakthroughs. I learned to forgive myself for the mistakes I had made, recognizing that growth often comes from embracing our imperfections. Therapy became an essential part of my journey, providing a safe space to explore my feelings and gain insight into my behaviors.

Through these sessions, I began to dismantle the walls I had built around my heart, allowing vulnerability to coexist with strength.

With time, I also started to rebuild my relationship with my daughter's mother. While we faced difficulties, we recognized the importance of co-parenting and putting our daughter's needs first. Communication improved, and we learned to navigate the complexities of our relationship with respect and understanding. This shift not only benefited our daughter but also provided us both with a sense of closure and the possibility of friendship.

As I approached my mid-twenties, I could finally see the fruits of my labor. The darkness that had once enveloped me began to dissipate, replaced by a sense of clarity and purpose. I was no longer defined solely by my past mistakes; I had emerged as a resilient individual with a vision for the future. My daughter became my greatest motivator, inspiring me to strive for excellence in all aspects of my life.

Looking back, I realized that my journey was not just about overcoming obstacles; it was about embracing the transformative power of love, resilience, and self-discovery. Each chapter of my life had played a crucial role in shaping me into the person I had become. I had learned that life is not linear; it is a series of twists and turns, each contributing to our growth.

As I continued to write, I documented my journey, hoping to inspire others who might find themselves in similar situations. I wanted to share the message that healing is possible, that our past does not define us, and that we have the power to create a brighter future. Through vulnerability, connection, and self-reflection, we can navigate the complexities of life and emerge stronger than ever.

In the end, I understood that the journey of awakening is ongoing. There will always be challenges to face and lessons to learn, but I felt equipped to handle whatever came my way. With each passing day, I embraced the opportunity to grow, to love, and to be the best version of myself. The story continues, and I am ready to write the next chapter.

Chapter 5 *The Weight of Rebellion and Redemption*

My bishop preached countless messages about not allowing anything to separate you from the love of God. He would often tell me, "Ken, God wants a man." This declaration resonated with me, yet it also troubled me deeply.

I often felt uncomfortable when he referred to me as a preacher, especially during my teenage years. While he meant well, his words felt like an expectation I wasn't sure I could fulfill. He would sometimes put us to the test by having us read scripture or pray aloud, reminding us that we belonged to God. My struggle was knowing that I belonged to God while simultaneously yearning to indulge in the pleasures of the world.

I told myself I wanted to do what I wanted, when I wanted, and how I wanted. Little did I know, I would soon experience firsthand what rebellion against God truly felt like. I've always believed that when we disobey God or stray from our divine calling, we essentially invite struggle into our lives. And that's exactly what I did.

After enduring the heartbreak of my daughter's mother, I thought I was beginning to turn a corner. I had left the military, secured a job, and enrolled in school, all while trying to rebuild my life. During this time, I began to take an interest in a woman who was a little over ten years older than I was. She was kind, mature, and came from a good family. As time passed, we welcomed a daughter together. I loved her deeply and thought she was an amazing woman. She acted as a girlfriend while also nurturing me in many ways. She cooked for me, cleaned for me, and ensured I had everything I needed.

However, in the back of my mind, I still wrestled with my past relationship and the uncertainty of my future. I was still young and felt the urge to live life to the fullest; I wanted to party, date, and explore my youth. Despite my feelings for her, I didn't want to lose my freedom. She would often ask me if she was going to be a single woman forever, pressing the idea of marriage into our conversations. I felt torn. I loved her, yet I was also striving to define who "Ken was".

Eventually, I surrendered to her desire for commitment. We got engaged and eventually married. But let me be honest: I struggled with our age difference. Sometimes, when we were in public and shared moments of affection, we would receive strange looks from onlookers. This anxiety lingered, but I was willing to overlook it.

While we were married, we encountered several challenges. I struggled to fully commit to the marriage, and my interest in other women lingered in the back of my mind. Although I never acted on those impulses, the temptation was always present.

We lacked a firm foundation for our marriage. We didn't attend church regularly or establish a bond with God that was essential for our relationship. I didn't understand what it meant to be the man of my house, the one to offer spiritual direction. I knew I belonged to God, but I didn't know how to guide my family toward Him.

My first daughter came to stay with us for a while, but after some time, her mother wanted her back. I wanted my daughter to stay with me and my first wife, but she preferred that our daughter return to her mother. This disagreement became a significant turning point in our relationship. We began to argue daily, and she would often say, "If you don't like it, you can get out." Ironically, that comment didn't deter me; it almost felt like an invitation.

One day, after another argument, I took her words to heart and moved out while she was at work. I found an apartment in a building owned by a good friend of my brother's. It was a studio apartment, and in my mind, it was finally my time to do what I wanted. I started working for an insurance company on the north side of Chicago, feeling liberated as I embraced my newfound independence.

However, I was still young and wanted to sow my wild oats. I began partying regularly, sometimes coming home so late that I'd barely have time to change clothes before heading to work again.

My attendance suffered, and I received several warnings about being late. Ultimately, my lack of responsibility led to my termination. I figured I could collect unemployment until I figured things out, but soon enough, I received a letter stating I was ineligible because I had been terminated for poor attendance.

This hit me hard. I now had two daughters to care for, and I felt tremendous pressure. My rent started to fall behind, and although I explained my situation to my landlord, a friend of my brother's, he could only advise me to do my best.

Just when I thought I had a chance to turn things around, I noticed that my car had been booted due to unpaid parking tickets. This unfortunate turn of events prevented me from going to a job interview I had lined up.

Feeling too ashamed to ask my family for help, I tried to figure things out on my own. The following day, I called the city pound to pick up my car, only to discover it was gone. The finance company had paid the tickets and repossessed it.

Here I was, a father to two daughters, with no money, no income, and now no car. My rent was overdue, and my car had been taken away. To make matters worse, I learned that a woman I casually dated was pregnant, and the child could potentially be mine. I struggled to accept this reality due to the nature of our involvement.

Additionally, I was battling a gambling addiction, often using the little money I had to gamble at the boats. I would even gamble my rent money, putting myself in a precarious financial situation. I fell into a dark place and withdrew from everyone, even my brothers, who were trying to check on me.

One day, they came by my apartment and rang the bell repeatedly. I was in such a dark place that I felt like I wanted to end it all. In a moment of desperation, I stuck my head out the window with a gun to my head and told them if they rang the bell one more time, I would kill myself. My brothers, filled with anguish, cried out for me to let them help.

In that moment, I had a supernatural experience. God asked me, "Are you tired?" and I replied, "Yes, Lord, I'm tired." At that moment,

I felt that my brothers were crying out to God on my behalf. When I finally put the gun down, I let them in, and they consoled me. I opened up about everything that was happening in my life. They assured me that we were family and that we would get through this together.

About a week later, I found a job, and I was able to catch up on my rent. I started attending church regularly and trying to take an active role in my faith. Yes, I still faced struggles, but this felt like a significant turning point.

By then, I was expecting baby number three—a boy. Shortly after his birth, his mother moved to Iowa. I attempted to work with her to raise our son, but our relationship was undefined and fraught with difficulties. This tumultuous experience highlighted the consequences of living life outside God's plan.

Looking back, I wished I could turn back time and make different choices. Life had dealt me a hand I had to play. I eventually moved back to my mother's house to help financially and save money, especially with three children to care for. I often wished I had a father figure around to guide me through my poor decisions.

During this time, I met a nice woman who had four children. She had moved to Chicago from Peoria after going through a divorce. As always, I found myself jumping from relationship to relationship, grappling with my personal battles. This woman was incredibly supportive, knowing when to offer her opinion and when to remain silent. There were days when I felt overwhelmed, and her silent presence was often the best therapy.

However, she faced her own challenges. She left her job for what turned out to be a pyramid scheme. One day, she called me, distressed because the job wasn't paying her what she had expected. I reminded her that I had warned her about the potential risks of such a position. Our conversation escalated into a heated argument. We hung up on each other, and for two days, she tried to reach me, but I ignored her calls, allowing my pride to get in the way.

On Sunday morning, I saw that I had missed her final call in the early hours. As I scrolled through her messages, I saw her pleas for reconciliation, affirming her love for me. But then I noticed a missed call from her brother, and his trembling voice informed me that she had died.

My heart shattered. I felt a deep sense of guilt, believing that if I had answered her calls, maybe her life could have been saved. After speaking with her brother, I learned that she had gone home for the weekend and had been shot during a robbery. I couldn't bring myself to attend her funeral; I was too distraught and overwhelmed with guilt.

In the days following her death, I tried to date other women, but I often found myself breaking down in tears, still haunted by her memory. One day, while getting to know someone new, I shared the story of my late girlfriend. As I became emotional, she reassured me, saying, "This is not your fault." Her compassion offered me a sense of closure and healing I desperately needed.

I held onto my faith, realizing that sometimes God uses others to help us heal. I yearned to move past the pain and trauma of my girlfriend's death, and I felt a new beginning was on the horizon. The journey was far from over, but I was beginning to understand that each struggle brought me closer to finding my true self and my place in God's plan.

Chapter 6- A New Season of Love, Loss, and Lessons

Life has a way of writing stories we never expect. My journey took a profound turn when a woman entered my life during one of my most challenging seasons. She stood by me after my girlfriend passed away, offering unwavering support that gradually blossomed into something deeper. Over time, our bond grew so strong that, after four months of dating, I proposed to her on her grandparents' 50th wedding anniversary.

It was a joyous moment that symbolized not only our love but also the hope of building a future together. Although we didn't set a firm wedding date, we began to intertwine our lives, moving in together and dreaming about what was ahead.

At the time, I was deeply invested in my work on Chicago's west side. My role involved overseeing a community program designed to empower men and women by teaching essential technology skills like basic computing, web design, and job readiness. These efforts aimed to bridge the digital divide in underserved communities. My passion for service extended beyond my job. One day, on a whim, I decided to purchase $20–$25 worth of school supplies—just enough to provide for 40 kids. What started as a small act of kindness evolved into the Alice Cooper Foundation, named in honor of my grandmother. Her legacy of compassion inspired me to continue giving back. Through this foundation, we organized annual back-to-school drives, providing supplies and hope to countless families.

Amid these efforts, life presented us with what seemed like a miraculous blessing. My fiancée and I learned we were expecting a baby boy. The news filled us with indescribable joy. We eagerly prepared for his arrival, decorating his nursery and filling his closet with tiny clothes.

But the joy was short-lived. During a routine appointment, we were devastated to learn that our son's heartbeat had stopped. Words cannot capture the depth of our heartbreak. My fiancée went into labor, and after several hours, she delivered our baby boy, Ken Jr. Though he never took a breath in this world, his presence left an indelible mark on our hearts.

We chose to honor Ken Jr.'s memory with a graveside service, surrounded by family. Though we didn't hold a formal funeral, the gathering provided a space to grieve and celebrate his brief but meaningful existence. The experience tested my faith in ways I hadn't anticipated, yet it also deepened my trust in God's sovereignty. In the midst of heartbreak, I leaned on Him for strength and direction, believing that even in loss, there was purpose.

Despite the sorrow, life eventually began to stabilize. My fiancée and I set a wedding date and celebrated our union surrounded by loved ones. Soon after, we welcomed a new blessing—our daughter, born in March 2008. To support her dream of being a stay-at-home mom, we sold our condo and moved in with her mother. Just over a year later, we were blessed with a second daughter. Although building a new home didn't materialize as we had hoped, we found a spacious house that perfectly suited our growing family. For a time, life felt stable and fulfilling.

However, as often happens, life threw unexpected challenges our way. My involvement in church had always been a significant part

of my life, but in this season, I felt a deeper calling to ministry. I became an assistant pastor,
but in hindsight, I didn't fully discuss this decision with my wife.

This lack of communication created strain in
our marriage, especially as we juggled financial pressures and the demands of raising two
young children.

During this period, God planted a vision in my
heart for a new ministry called 1 Walk Ministries. Stepping out in faith, I began hosting
church services in our kitchen. My wife, ever
practical, encouraged me to find a dedicated space for worship. After some searching, I rented a location an hour and forty
minutes away for just $40 a month. While the
arrangement allowed the ministry to grow, the
long commute added tension to an already
challenging season.

By 2012, 1 Walk Ministries was officially born.
The joy of following God's calling was

tempered by the realities of pastoring. My wife, in her honesty, expressed that she didn't feel ready for the weight of being a pastor's wife. She encouraged me to focus on motivational speaking instead, a path she believed would better align with our family's needs.

Her words, though painful to hear, forced me to reflect deeply on my priorities and the toll my decisions were taking on our marriage. Over time, the weight of these challenges proved too much, and we made the heartbreaking decision to divorce. It was a painful chapter not only for us but also for our families, who had invested so much in our union.

As if navigating a divorce wasn't difficult enough, life dealt another blow with the loss of my youngest brother. His infectious laughter and joyful spirit had been a cornerstone of our family. Losing him left a void that was felt deeply by all who knew him. In a short span of time, I went from living in a spacious 3,000-square-foot home to a modest 500-square-foot apartment. Balancing the responsibilities of pastoring, grieving, and healing felt over-whelming. I was embarrassed, angry, and deeply hurt, but I clung to the belief that God was still at work in my life.

Reflecting on my marriage, I've come to understand that sometimes two good people aren't necessarily good for each other. The end of our relationship didn't erase the love we shared or the good times we experienced together. Instead, it highlighted the complexities of life and the importance of communication, shared vision, and mutual support. While the pain of divorce was immense, I am grateful for the lessons it taught me and the growth it inspired.

Through these experiences, I've learned that life is a tapestry woven with threads of joy, sorrow, triumph, and failure. Each thread contributes to the bigger picture, revealing a masterpiece that only becomes clear in hindsight. The loss of my son, the end of my marriage, and the passing of my brother were all deeply painful, but they also shaped me into a person with greater empathy, resilience, and faith.

The journey has not been easy, but it has been purposeful. The Alice Cooper Foundation continues to serve as a beacon of hope in the community, embodying the values my grandmother instilled in me. 1 Walk Ministries, though born from humble beginnings, remains a testament to God's ability to use imperfect people to fulfill His perfect plan. And though my personal life has had its share of ups and downs, I am reminded daily that every challenge is an opportunity to grow closer to the person God has called me to be.

As I look to the future, I carry with me the lessons of the past. Love, loss, and resilience are not isolated experiences but interconnected chapters of a larger story. They remind me to cherish the moments of joy, to seek purpose in the midst of pain, and to trust that God is always at work, even when life feels uncertain. My journey is far from over, but I am committed to embracing each new chapter with faith, hope, and gratitude.

Chapter 7 The Journey of a Single Pastor in Ministry

Navigating the path of ministry as a single pastor has been one of the most challenging yet transformative experiences of my life. Growing up, I only ever saw pastors who were married, leading ministries with the support of a spouse by their side. When I entered ministry, I assumed my journey would follow the same pattern. However, life had other plans, and by the time my divorce was finalized, I found myself standing at the helm of a church alone.

It was a new and unsettling reality, one that forced me to confront my doubts, insecurities, and faith in ways I never expected.

The finalization of my divorce coincided with an exciting milestone for our ministry: moving into a new location. The move was a symbol of growth and progress, yet personally, I felt anything but victorious. I will never forget the crushing sense of defeat I experienced during my first year in ministry.

One Sunday stands out vividly in my memory—only Deacon Bell and I showed up for worship. The small room we rented could hold just 15 people, but that morning, it felt cavernously empty.

Despite my frustration, Deacon Bell insisted on going through every part of the service, including the offering. I watched in disbelief as he carried the offering tray to each empty chair, pausing as if someone were sitting there. My initial annoyance quickly gave way to a profound lesson.

God used that moment to remind me of the power of faith—to call things into existence as though they already were. Deacon Bell was moving in faith, declaring growth and vitality for our ministry even when it seemed hopeless.

That day, I learned that ministry doesn't have to start big; it just has to be real. From that point forward, I committed to trusting God's plan, no matter how things looked.

 Ministry is both a privilege and a challenge. While it builds your spiritual "muscles," it also exposes you to scrutiny and pressure. As a single pastor, I faced relentless opinions, especially from fellow pastors, about how my marital status would hinder my ministry. Their comments planted seeds of doubt in my mind, and the weight of their expectations felt unbearable at times.

Simultaneously, I was battling my own feelings of loss and loneliness. Divorce is like a death—it leaves a void that takes time to heal. For years, I had been accustomed to having a partner by my side, someone to share life's joys and burdens. Adjusting to singlehood was a painful and unfamiliar process.

Amid the pressure to remarry and the ache of loneliness, I reconnected with a childhood friend who had been a source of encouragement during my divorce. She was kind, genuine, and deeply spiritual—a prayer warrior who truly wanted the best for me. As we spent time together, our relationship quickly escalated, and soon we were discussing marriage.

Despite her wisdom and insistence on taking things slow, I pushed forward. I was desperate to silence the voices around me and fulfill the image of a married pastor. We got engaged, received counseling, and eventually married. Initially, things seemed promising, but I quickly realized the consequences of rushing ahead without discernment.

We hadn't taken the time to truly know and understand each other. While we shared a love for God and ministry, we lacked the foundation necessary for a lasting marriage.

Our union ended amicably, but it was my third divorce—a reality that left me feeling like a complete failure. I questioned why God would use someone like me, with all my flaws and mistakes, to lead His people. Yet once again, God reminded me that my struggles were part of His plan to equip me for greater purpose. He used this season to thicken my skin and deepen my reliance on Him.

Through these trials, God began to reshape my vision for ministry. A pivotal moment came during a conversation with a friend, who re-marked that church should be a place for community—a space where people can build character, morals, and integrity. This insight sparked a revelation: our ministry would become Social Center International Ministries, a place for family, community, and all people.

God also revealed that our reach would extend beyond the local community, impacting lives on both national and international levels. This new vision reinvigorated our efforts, and we expanded our outreach initiatives. From school supply drives and job fairs to midnight prayer vigils and homeless advocacy, we became a cornerstone of hope and support in Chicago and beyond.

Even during the COVID-19 pandemic, our ministry adapted to provide a safe space for worship and connection. Our work gained recognition, and the name Apostle Ken Fuller began to resonate across neighborhoods and social media platforms. Yet, through it all, I remained grounded in the understanding that our success was rooted in God's faithfulness, not my own efforts.

The journey of healing after my third divorce was neither quick nor easy. I sought counseling to address the trauma I had carried for years, determined to break the cycle of pain and poor decision-making. This process not only helped me heal but also equipped me to lead with greater empathy and wisdom.

What stood out most during this time was the unwavering support of my congregation. They prayed for both my ex-wife and me, demonstrating the love and grace that should define the church. Their encouragement reminded me that God's calling on my life had not changed, even in the face of personal failure.

I also learned the critical importance of waiting on God and allowing time for relationships to develop naturally. Rushing ahead, whether in marriage or ministry, often leads to unnecessary pain. Discernment and patience are vital for building healthy, lasting connections.

 Throughout my journey, one scripture has been a constant source of strength: Jeremiah 29:11—*"For I know the plans I have for you,"* declares the Lord, *"plans to prosper you and not to harm you, plans to give you hope and a future."* This promise has carried me through moments of doubt and despair, reminding me that failure is not an option when God is in control.

I may have stumbled along the way, but each challenge has refined me, shaping me into a pastor who leads with intention and humility. Today, I am more committed than ever to following the Holy Spirit's guidance and serving with integrity.

Social Center International Ministries continues to grow, both in scope and impact. We remain dedicated to being a place of hope, healing, and community. From feeding the homeless to interceding for the streets of Chicago, our mission is rooted in the belief that God's love transforms lives.

My journey as a single pastor has been anything but conventional, but it has been undeniably purposeful. Each trial, each failure, and each victory has deepened my faith and strengthened my resolve to fulfill God's calling. To anyone reading this, know that your struggles do not disqualify you. If anything, they prepare you for greater impact. Trust the process, and remember: *failure is not an option.*

Chapter 8 Faithing Through: Leading Through the Storm

In 2019, life and ministry seemed to be flourishing. I was beginning to feel a profound sense of purpose in my pastoral role, understanding the true meaning of being a shepherd. Ministry, I often tell people, is not for the faint of heart. It can be a thankless task, filled with moments of sacrifice and challenges that require an unshakable trust in God's will. Yet, through it all, I had started to hear God's voice in ways I could hardly explain. His whispers became a profound guide, and I knew He was preparing me for something greater.

In that year, God gave me a vision—a vision of a calamity that would affect the entire world, a trauma that would challenge our faith like never before. It wasn't a faint impression; it was clear and direct. The Lord revealed to me that the body of Christ would be tested, stretched to its limits.

In response, He gave me a message to preach titled *"Faithing Through."* The central message was simple yet profound: possessing faith wasn't going to be enough. Whatever was coming would require an ongoing, resilient, and evolving faith to endure both the event and its aftermath.

This word of warning was heavy on my heart, but I obeyed. I preached the message with fervor, although I felt a deep concern about what this vision might mean. By the end of 2019, murmurs about an illness called COVID-19 began to emerge. Reports suggested it originated overseas, but no one could have predicted the global upheaval it would bring. At first, the news felt distant—a concern but not an immediate threat. That changed quickly as fear swept across the globe.

By early 2020, COVID-19 had become a worldwide crisis. Anxiety gripped nations, and uncertainty hovered like a storm cloud. The unthinkable happened: the virus reached the United States. The fear was palpable, and life as we knew it began to unravel. The government issued mandates that shuttered businesses, schools, and churches. Social distancing, masks, and rigorous hand sanitation became the new normal.

At the same time, our ministry had acquired a new location on the southeast side of Chicago, and we were in the midst of renovations. We were excitedly preparing for a grand opening when the pandemic disrupted everything. The world was shutting down, and plans were put on indefinite hold. People were afraid, their faith shaken, and the weight of their questions fell squarely on the shoulders of pastors and leaders like myself.

I vividly remember the countless phone calls. People were grieving, uncertain, and overwhelmed. Loved ones were falling ill, and hospitals became inaccessible. Family members couldn't be with their sick or dying loved ones. Funerals were reduced to brief, distanced gatherings or avoided altogether. The world felt like one long, unending funeral.

For my family, the pandemic brought its own challenges. My mother fell gravely ill, and we feared the worst. When she was hospitalized, the doctors initially claimed she had COVID-19. That diagnosis was later refuted, but the experience tested our faith to its core. Long before the pandemic, she had faced severe health challenges, and I'll never forget standing by her bedside during one of those moments.

She was so weak, and I could hardly hold back my tears as I leaned over and whispered, *"Mom, it's me. I still need you."* Despite her condition, God gave her the strength to look at me and convey something profound. Without speaking, her eyes said, *"Son, be strong."* That moment was a testament to the power of God's presence—a presence she had introduced us to many years ago. I'm thankful to say that God brought her through that storm and the trials of the pandemic as well.

 As a pastor, navigating this pandemic was unlike anything I had ever experienced. Churches were forced to close their doors, shifting to online services or limited in-person gatherings. Some ministers defied government orders and faced arrests, arguing that shutting down worship violated the separation of church and state.

For many of us, the pandemic forced a realization: the gospel isn't confined to the walls of a building. Ministry became more innovative and far-reaching as pastors embraced technology and found new ways to connect with their congregations. Personally, this was a significant challenge for me. I had resisted the idea of an online presence, firmly believing that worship belonged in the sanctuary. But COVID-19 forced me to adapt, and it

stretched my faith in ways I hadn't anticipated.

God reminded me of the message He had given me in 2019: *"Faithing Through."* This was the time to live it out, to walk by faith and lead others to do the same. When the renovations on our new location were complete, I didn't pressure anyone to return to the sanctuary. In-stead, the congregation approached me, ea-ger to gather again in worship. We followed every CDC guideline, stayed in constant prayer, and trusted God. To His glory, not a sin-gle member contracted COVID-19 during our services.

The pandemic brought emotional and spiritual weight that was difficult to bear, but it also deepened my understanding of God's pur-pose. I often asked God, "Why? What is the purpose of all this?" His answer was clear: *"You can't lead people through something you've never been through yourself."*

This revelation transformed my perspective. The pandemic was a crucible—a time of refining and preparation. It taught me to trust God in the unknown and to shepherd others through their darkest valleys. Our ministry didn't just survive the pandemic; it grew stronger. We provided food and resources to the community, supported one another, and strengthened our bonds as a church family.

However, the aftermath of the pandemic left scars. Many people never fully recovered from their losses—be it loved ones, jobs, or a sense of normalcy. Grief lingered, and for some, faith wavered. Yet, through it all, God remained faithful.

The experience of pastoring through COVID-19 was transformative. It taught me the value of obedience, resilience, and unwavering trust in God's plan. It reminded me that ministry is about more than sermons and services—it's about serving people in their most desperate moments and pointing them to the hope found in Christ.

As I reflect on that season, I'm reminded of the hymn that declares, *"What a mighty God we serve."* Indeed, He is mighty. He carried us through one of the most challenging times in modern history and revealed His power, presence, and purpose in the process.

The message of "Faithing Through" remains as relevant today as it was then. Life will always bring challenges, but with ongoing faith, we can endure anything. The storms may rage, but God's promises are steadfast. Through it all, He reminds us that He is with us, guiding us, and preparing us for greater things ahead.

Chapter 9: Turbulence and Faith: A Pastor's Journey Through Crisis

I would never, under any circumstance, purposefully cause harm to another person. As a pastor and a believer in the sanctity of human life, I am a lover of all people, regardless of race, creed, color, or how they choose to identify. However, living in a city like Chicago, especially during the pandemic, challenged my principles. The city saw a sharp rise in violent crimes, including carjackings and robberies.

For years, I had steered clear of owning or carrying a weapon. I've always been an advocate against violence and crime, yet I understood the importance of protecting myself, my home, and those I love in the face of danger. One particular encounter cemented my decision to prepare for self-defense.

One night, while returning from a friend's house, I was approached by a man wielding a weapon. He intended to harm or rob me, but I stood firm and calmly told him that whatever he planned to do would not be a good idea.

After a tense exchange, he mumbled a few words, turned away, and left. Though I had escaped unscathed, I was shaken. The incident stayed with me and made me realize the need to protect myself better.

Soon after, I enrolled in a concealed carry class. While my intentions were clear—protection, not harm—I knew this decision carried a heavy burden. As a pastor, I loved God's people and would never want to harm another human being. Nevertheless, I felt compelled to ensure I could safeguard myself and others if faced with a life-threatening situation.

Even after acquiring a weapon, I didn't carry it daily. Most days, I left it at home, opting instead to trust my surroundings. However, I would take it with me if I traveled through areas I deemed less safe.

Sunday, January 10, 2021, is a day etched in my memory forever. It began as a joyous occasion. My ministry was celebrating my birthday during our Sunday service. As part of the celebration, some of the brothers in the church and I had built a replica of an airplane to accompany a sermon titled *"Prepare for Takeoff."* The airplane, complete with windows for participants to look out, symbolized the journey of faith and resilience.

The message was one of encouragement. I shared with the congregation that, like airplanes facing turbulence during flights, believers would encounter challenges in life. However, by staying rooted in the Word of God, they could overcome obstacles and reach the promises awaiting them. The sanctuary was filled with a palpable energy, and the presence of God could be felt throughout the service.

As the service progressed, I invited members to board the plane symbolically. Each time someone stepped up, I declared, "Prepare for takeoff." It was a prophetic and powerful moment that resonated with everyone in attendance. Toward the end of the service, a prophetic voice in the ministry approached me, asking to speak a word over my life. I agreed, and the prophet shared that God was preparing me for incredible blessings but warned that turbulence would come before takeoff.

Little did I know, that turbulence would begin almost immediately.

As I was wrapping up the service, I noticed a commotion near the door. One of the pastors informed me that several individuals, unaffiliated with our church, had arrived to confront a member of the congregation. These individuals were agitated and had apparently left before the police arrived earlier. However, they had now returned, and tensions were rising.

I instructed the pastor to call the police again, as it was clear the situation was escalating. Meanwhile, a member who had recently undergone open-heart surgery was outside amidst the disturbance. My concern for their safety grew, and I insisted on bringing them inside while waiting for the authorities.

By this time, most attendees had left, leaving only the core group of people who usually stayed behind after service. Despite my nervousness and racing heart, I opened the door cautiously, asking security and the recovering member to come inside. Unfortunately, the individuals outside became belligerent, demanding entry into the sanctuary.

I repeatedly told them this was a place of worship and that any personal grievances they had with our member needed to be addressed elsewhere. Despite my efforts to de-escalate, they attempted to force their way in. Acting quickly, I closed the door to keep them out.

The situation seemed to calm momentarily, but when I reopened the door to bring more people inside, one of the individuals appeared to have a weapon. As they flinched and moved toward the door, I reacted instinctively. In a split-second decision, I drew my weapon and fired a single warning shot into the air.

My heart pounded as I was pulled back inside by security. The individuals outside continued their attempts to force their way in, but by then, the police had arrived. Once they were on the scene, we explained the situation and the police reviewed security footage to understand clarity on what had transpired.

After reviewing the footage, the responding sergeant approached me. He acknowledged that he understood why I had acted as I did. However, he also informed me that firing a warning shot in the city of Chicago is illegal. Despite my intentions, I was taken into custody.

As I sat in the back of the police car, my mind raced. I thought about my congregation, my children who had witnessed the incident, and my mother, who I knew would be deeply worried. Tears streamed down the faces of those present at the church. Many of my leaders were outraged, feeling that the law was unfairly punishing the victim rather than the aggressors.

Despite their frustration, I urged the ministry to remain calm and focus on securing legal representation. Though I knew my actions were rooted in a desire to protect, I couldn't shake the shame and doubt that crept into my heart. I questioned how I had found myself in this situation and how it would impact my ministry and family.

That night, as I sat alone in a holding cell, I reflected on the turbulence the prophet had spoken of earlier that day. It was clear I was now in the midst of it. However, I also knew that God's Word offered hope and guidance in even the darkest valleys.

In the weeks that followed, I leaned heavily on my faith. The incident served as a humbling reminder of the unpredictability of life and the importance of staying grounded in God's promises. Though the legal process was arduous, I trusted that God would see me through.

The situation also deepened my understanding of protection and self-defense. While my intentions were noble, the consequences of my actions highlighted the complexities of navigating such decisions. As a pastor, I had always advocated for peace and nonviolence, and I had to reconcile this moment with those principles.

Ultimately, this experience strengthened my resolve to serve my community with greater compassion and wisdom. It reminded me that, as believers, we are not exempt from trials, but we are equipped with the tools to overcome them.

January 10, 2021, will forever remain a pivotal moment in my life. It was a day that tested my faith, my character, and my commitment to the calling God placed on my life. While the turbulence was challenging, it also served as a catalyst for growth and reflection.

As I continue my journey, I hold onto the message I shared with my congregation that day: "Prepare for takeoff." Life's challenges may shake us, but if we remain steadfast in our faith, we can soar to heights we never imagined. Though the path may be uncertain and the turbulence strong, the destination God has prepared for us is worth every trial we face along the way.

Chapter 10 But God A Journey of Pain, Purpose, and Resilience

I never would've thought in a million years that on January 11, 2021—the day after worship and the day before my birthday—I would wake up in a jail cell. The night before, countless supporters had gathered outside the jail, concerned for my well-being. Their presence left such an impression that one of the officers remarked, "You know a lot of people—so many have come to check on you."

Despite my circumstances, the officers were kind and treated me with respect, even offering guidance because they recognized that my intentions were pure. I sent word through one of the officers, asking those gathered outside to return home, assuring them that I was all right.

The night in jail was cold and lonely. But it was also an opportunity for reflection. I thought about the Apostle Paul, who found himself imprisoned, yet wrote some of his most profound letters during those dark moments.

In Philippians 4:4, Paul urges believers to *"Rejoice in the Lord always. I will say it again: Rejoice!"* Later in the same chapter, he declares in verse 12, *"I have learned the secret of being content in any and every situation, whether well fed or hungry, whether living in plenty or in want. I can do all things through Christ who strengthens me."*

As I sat in that cell, I clung to those words. I began to pray, speaking directly to God, because I knew deep down that this was not the end of my story. Every trial has a lesson, but the question is whether we choose to learn from it.

The next morning, I was taken to court, where an attorney—a remarkable woman of God with a passion for justice—was hired to represent me. She was my advocate, fighting on my behalf, and by the grace of God, I was granted bail. The catch was that the bail had to be posted by 4:30 PM that same day. After the hearing, I was returned to my cell, which I shared with men of various races and backgrounds.

As the hours passed, some of the men shared their stories—some admitted to their crimes, while others proclaimed their innocence. I didn't know what to believe, but I realized it wasn't my place to judge. Salvation, I reminded myself, is available to all who seek it, regardless of their past. God gave me the opportunity to minister to a few of them.

I didn't tell them I was a pastor—not out of shame, but because I wanted them to speak freely without feeling judged. The Apostle Paul's words echoed in my mind: *"I have become all things to all people so that by all possible means I might save some"* (1 Corinthians 9:22). Jesus Himself lived among the broken, understanding their struggles. I sought to follow His example.

As the clock inched closer to 4:30 PM, my anxiety grew. If my bail wasn't posted in time, I'd face another night—or more—in jail. At 4:15 PM, I still hadn't heard anything. Tears welled up in my eyes. The officers began moving us to general population, where I would be processed like any other inmate.

In line with other men, I watched as they were fitted with uniforms marked with the acronym *IDOC* which stands for *"Illinois Department of Corrections."* When it was my turn, I was handed brown clothing and I put on the pants, but they didn't fit. The officers gave me another pair of pants, then another, but none were the right size. As I struggled to pull them on, an officer across the room called out my name: "Fuller, your bail has been posted." It was 4:26 PM.

I couldn't hold back the tears any longer. They streamed down my face as I thanked God for delivering me. One of the officers, noticing my tears, consoled me. "Come on, my brother," he said. "Let's get you out of here."

As I prepared to leave, a fellow whispered a number to me and asked that I call his fiancé to let her know where he was at. He said, let her know I'm okay." I promised him I would. To my surprise, as I sat in the waiting area, the same man was released shortly after me. "You remembered the number," he said, astonished. I smiled, knowing that God had extended grace to both of us that day.

That night, I went straight to my mother's house. We embraced, crying tears of relief and gratitude. "Mom," I told her, "all is well."

Afterward, I returned home, eager to sleep in my own bed.

The next day was my birthday, but instead of celebrating, I got to work. I met with my attorney to discuss the case. She warned me that the road ahead would be long and challenging, but I was determined to fight for my name and my freedom. Each court appearance was an emotional rollercoaster, filled with anxiety and uncertainty. I saw people sentenced to years in prison, their lives forever changed.

At times, I fell into despair. Before my arrest, I had been planning to purchase a laundromat, a beauty supply store, and a nail salon. Those dreams were now on hold as my resources were drained by legal fees. By December 2021, the state offered me a plea deal that included jail time. I advised my attorney to reject it as I wanted to clear my name. Together, we decided to fight.

Through it all, I continued preaching, teaching, and spreading the gospel. Like Paul, I refused to let my circumstances silence me. My social media following grew exponentially as I shared messages of hope and resilience. I led seminars, developed leaders, and even became a columnist for a local magazine. Despite the storm I was in, I remained committed to my calling.

By March 2022, the state was adamant: they wanted me to serve jail time. Unable to reach an agreement, we prepared for trial in May 2022. The pressure was immense, but I clung to my faith. Jeremiah 29:11 became my anchor: *"For I know the plans I have for you,"* declares the Lord, *"plans to prosper you and not to harm you, plans to give you hope and a future."*

When the trial finally arrived, I was weary but resolute. As the judge prepared to render his verdict, I stood in the courtroom surrounded by my attorney, my leadership team, and other supporters. The judge's words were like music to my ears: "Not guilty." The charges were dropped.

A silent praise erupted in the courtroom. Tears streamed down my face as I walked out, free at last. All I could do was give God the glory for what He had done.

This is why I titled my story *But God*. It is a testament to pain, purpose, and resilience. Some of the pain I experienced was self-inflicted, but God's grace carried me through. No matter the trials we face, we must remember that our story doesn't end in the storm—it ends in the *but God*.

I pray that my journey inspires you to persevere through life's challenges. People may doubt you, circumstances may seem insurmountable but remember: it's not about what happens to you; it's about how you respond. Never forget the power of *But God*.

This is my story.